ONE MAN SHOW

by

Frank Asch

photographs by

Jan Asch

Richard C. Owen Publishers, Inc.
Katonah, New York

Meet the Author titles

Verna Aardema *A Bookworm Who Hatched*
David A. Adler *My Writing Day*
Frank Asch *One Man Show*
Joseph Bruchac *Seeing the Circle*
Eve Bunting *Once Upon a Time*
Lynne Cherry *Making a Difference in the World*
Lois Ehlert *Under My Nose*
Jean Fritz *Surprising Myself*
Paul Goble *Hau Kola Hello Friend*
Ruth Heller *Fine Lines*
Lee Bennett Hopkins *The Writing Bug*
James Howe *Playing with Words*
Johanna Hurwitz *A Dream Come True*

Karla Kuskin *Thoughts, Pictures, and Words*
Thomas Locker *The Man Who Paints Nature*
Jonathan London *Tell Me a Story*
George Ella Lyon *A Wordful Child*
Margaret Mahy *My Mysterious World*
Rafe Martin *A Storyteller's Story*
Patricia McKissack *Can You Imagine?*
Patricia Polacco *Firetalking*
Laurence Pringle *Nature! Wild and Wonderful*
Cynthia Rylant *Best Wishes*
Seymour Simon *From Paper Airplanes to Outer Space*
Jean Van Leeuwen *Growing Ideas*
Jane Yolen *A Letter from Phoenix Farm*

Richard C. Owen Publishers, Inc.
PO Box 585
Katonah, New York 10536

Library of Congress Cataloging-in-Publication Data

Asch, Frank.
     One man show / by Frank Asch ; photographs by Jan Asch.
          p . cm . — (Meet the author)
      Summary: In this autobiographical account an author and illustrator of children's books shares his life, daily activities, and creative process, and shows how all are intertwined.
          ISBN 1-57274-095-7
          1. Asch, Frank—Biography—Juvenile literature.
2. Authors, American—20th century—Biography—Juvenile literature.
3. Children's literature—Authorship— Juvenile literature
[1. Asch, Frank. 2. Authors, American. 3. Illustrators.]
I. Asch, Jan, ill. II. Title. III. Series: Meet the author
(Katonah, N.Y.)
PS3551.S3Z47 1997
813' .54—dc21
[B]   97-7626

Editorial, Art, and Production Director *Janice Boland*
Production Assistant *Donna Parsons*
Color separations by Leo P. Callahan Inc., Binghamton, NY

Printed in the United States of America

9 8 7 6 5 4

To Roy then and now

I love making children's books.
But I didn't always want to be
a children's book author and illustrator.
When I was young I just wanted
to blow bubbles, swing on swings, and daydream.

One of the things I dreamed about
was becoming a cowboy like Roy Rogers.
He was my hero. I loved the way he rode
his horse Trigger, and always got the bad guys.
He was tough, but kind and good.

By the time I reached high school
I wanted to be an artist.

Only I didn't think I had much talent.
Then something happened that changed my life.
One day I walked into my high school art class
and saw an entire bulletin board covered
with my art work. Above the bulletin board
my art teacher had written:
Frank Asch: One Man Show.
From then on, I began to think that
maybe someday I really could become an artist.
But I wasn't sure what kind of artist I wanted to be.

After high school I went to an art school in
New York City called Cooper Union.
What a change that was!
I grew up, with my older brother and sister,
in the country where I had a forest to play in.
Now I was living in a forest of skyscrapers.
When I was in Cooper Union I spent a lot of
time with my Uncle Crecenzo.
He had a small carpentry shop on
Thomson Street in Greenwich Village.

Uncle Crecenzo was always making up
games and stories for the neighborhood kids.

Though I learned a lot from my teachers
at Cooper Union, I learned even more
from my uncle.

Playing with Uncle Crecenzo
and the kids on Thomson Street
made me realize I didn't want my art
to hang in museums. I wanted to make art for kids.
I wrote my first children's book
when I was still an art student at Cooper Union.
It was called *George's Store*.
It was really about my Uncle Crecenzo.

After art school I traveled to India where I taught
English and studied yoga. When I returned to
the United States, I met my future wife Jan.
We were married and taught in a Montessori school
in New Jersey. After a year of teaching,
Jan and I started our own children's theatre.
We called it *The Belly Buttons*. We made puppets
and put on shows. Jan sang songs.
It was a great way to try out new stories.

Then we moved to New England and our son
Devin was born. Becoming a father was one of the
most wonderful things that ever happened to me!
I loved watching Devin explore the world.
Everything was new to him.

It was then that I started writing books about
Moon Bear and Little Bird.

Like Devin when he was small,
Moon Bear is always learning about things
for the first time.

Jan and I loved being with Devin so much
that we educated him ourselves at home.
Devin had lots of other home-schooled children
to play with, and I got to play with them, too.

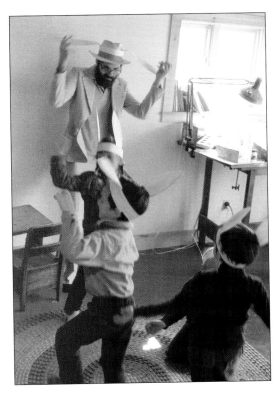

People often ask me where I get my ideas for my books.
For sure, I get some ideas from being with kids.
But I also get ideas from feelings I had
when I was a child. Some of those feelings
were not so pleasant, like anger and fear.
For years I tried to write a story
that would acknowledge children's fears
without making them worse.
The idea of how this could be done
came to me in a dream.

The book I wrote is called *Here Comes the Cat!*
The story is about a town of mice who seem to be
afraid of a sinister cat. But the cat turns out to be
the bearer of a giant piece of cheese!
The illustrator was Vladimir Vagin, a Russian citizen.
He now lives in America, in the same town as I.

The Earth and I are friends

Several years ago I started asking the children
who sent me letters to complete the phrase:
"The Earth and I . . ."
Most of them wrote back saying,
"The Earth and I are friends."
That one sentence became the core idea
for my book, *The Earth and I.*

Kids really love the Earth!

Another book I've written about the environment
is called *Water*. It suggests that we are all
like drops of water flowing to the sea.

Lately I've been working with Ted Levin,
a photographer and naturalist.

Ted and I have canoed in the Everglades,
traveled to the desert, and camped in the Arctic
with walruses and bears.

When I'm with Ted in a new place,
I feel like I'm seeing the Earth for the first time.
Ted shares his fierce love of nature with me.
Then I turn my experiences and feelings into
poems to go with his dazzling photographs.
We're currently working on our third book,
called *Caribou Poems*.

Not all of my ideas come from being in far-off places.
I live in Middletown Springs, Vermont.

One day, from my studio window I saw a fawn
walking through a cow pasture. I thought,
"What would happen if that fawn met a calf?
Could they become friends?
What could they do together that would
be interesting? And what would it mean?"
That last question is the most important one of all.
When I can answer it, I know I have a story
with a beginning, a middle, and most importantly,
an end. That idea ended up as a book called
Oats and Wild Apples.

It's fun to write and illustrate books!
But it can be hard work. Sometimes you have to work
word by word, line by line, dot by dot, thinking about
every change you make. Some of my stories take years
to complete. Some come in a flash. I used to write
out my stories in pen or pencil. Now I use a computer.
When I'm working on a poetry book
I keep a small notebook in my pocket.
When I see something that gives me an idea
or a feeling, I write it down.
Later I go over these ideas and develop them
on the computer. For a picture book, I often work
on the story and the pictures at the same time.

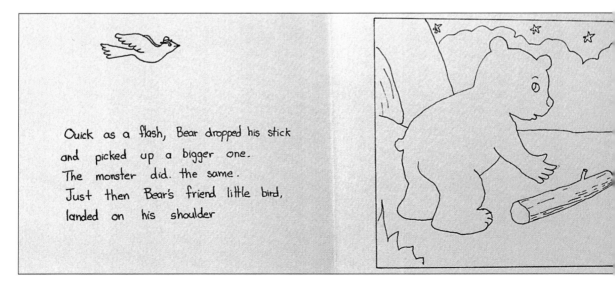

Quick as a flash, Bear dropped his stick
and picked up a bigger one.
The monster did. the same.
Just then Bear's friend little bird,
landed on his shoulder

When I'm stuck for an idea, I think hard—
then I go outdoors. I chop wood, play with kids,
or fly a kite. If that doesn't work I take a nap
and look for solutions in dreams.

When I'm having trouble with a drawing
I scribble on tracing paper.
Then I look into my scribbles for a new image.

My early art was mostly black and white.

Now my work is full of color, and often broad and simple.

I want kids to look at my art and think, "Hey, I can do that!"

I start by sketching.

Then I use a light box to redraw my pictures.

I used to illustrate all my books with acrylics and watercolors.

Now I also create my pictures with a computer.

I don't have a typical day.
But if you were to visit me,
you might find me working
upstairs in my studio,
or outside with one of our horses,
or with my dog Robi,

or I might be looking for heart-shaped rocks,
which I collect.

When I'm not working
on a new book,
I visit schools where I
put on my Moon Bear
costume and tell
stories.

And when I have time, I do art or make up stories
with the home-schooled kids in town.
Sometimes we put on puppet shows for the school kids.
And sometimes we just blow bubbles,
swing on swings, and daydream.

Other Books by Frank Asch

Cactus Poems; *Dear Brother*; *Hands around Lincoln School*;
Happy Birthday Moon; *Last Puppy*; *Little Fish, Big Fish*;
Moondance; *Moon Bear's Books*; *Moon Bear's Pet*, *Sawgrass Poems*

About the Photographer

Jan Asch enjoys photography,
weaving, gardening, swimming, and
horses. As well as helping her
husband Frank Asch with his many
projects, Jan has published children's
stories and songs on her own. She is
currently working on a novel.

Acknowledgments

Photographs on pages 3 and 5 appear with the permission of The Roy Rogers-Dale Evans Museum, Victorville, California. Photographs on pages 4, 7, 10, 12, 13, 14, and 27 (top) courtesy of Frank Asch. Photograph on page 6 by Des McClean. Illustration on page 8 from *George's Store*, on page 15, on page 21 from *Oats and Apples*, on page 22 and 24, and illustration on page 25 from *Elvira Everything* by Frank Asch, appear courtesy of Frank Asch. Illustration on page 11 from *Moon Bear's Pet* by Frank Asch. Copyright 1997 by Frank Asch. Reprinted by permission of Simon & Schuster Books for Young Readers, an imprint of Simon & Schuster Children's Publishing Division. Cover of *Here Comes the Cat!* on page 14 by Frank Asch and Vladimir Vagin. Copyright 1989 by Frank Asch and Vladimir Vagin. Reprinted by permission of Scholastic Inc. Illustrations on page 16 from *The Earth and I*, ©1994 by Frank Asch. Reprinted by permission of Harcourt Brace & Company. Illustrations on page 17 from *Water*, ©1995 by Frank Asch. Reprinted by permission of Harcourt Brace & Company. Photographs on pages 18 and 19, by Ted Levin, appear courtesy of Ted Levin. Photographs on page 30 by Mike McKeen. Photograph on back cover of Frank Asch in Alaska with walruses by Ted Levin appears courtesy of Ted Levin.